MW01180951

AMAZING GRACE

by Eliza L. Bath

authorHOUSE®

AuthorHouse™
1663 Liberty Drive
Bloomington, IN 47403
www.authorhouse.com
Phone: 1-800-839-8640

First published by AuthorHouse   4/1/2010

ISBN: 978-1-4490-9216-0 (sc)
ISBN: 978-1-4490-9215-3 (hc)

Library of Congress Control Number: 2010902505

Printed in the United States of America
Bloomington, Indiana

This book is printed on acid-free paper.

Prayer for Renewal

Lord Jesus, as you call me to refocus my mind and heart on you, I ask you to work your wondrous gift of mercy and restore me to you. Renew my mind and guide my heart to be focused solely on you. May my sense of self-importance decrease and your divine image grow ever deeper in me.

Written September, 1952

Himself He Would Not Save

He could have saved himself
     If he wanted to,

But he hung there on the cruel cross
     For me and for you.

When Jesus, my Lord was crucified,
     "He saves others, but himself he could not save"

Is what the people cried.
     The people back then didn't realize
     It was for them he was crucified.

Today they're the same as they
     Were back then.

Satan has deafened their ears,
     Blinded their eyes
     So they cannot hear or see

Christ hanging on the cross
     Of Calvary

Saying "I will save any sinner
     That comes unto me."

Written March 12, 1970

2

My Old Friend

In memory of my old home on
Taylor Wells Rd.   February, 1983

Goodbye, old friend.
>   For many years you have sheltered and cared
>   For me and mine.

Though teardrops start,
>   You cannot know how much I'll miss you.

When I'm gone, you will
>   Always have a place in my heart.

I'll miss your love and protection forever,
>   The wind and snow and rain,.

And though we will never live in you again,
>   You will always be my friend.

The memories of you will bring tears of joy
>   Because you sheltered me,
>   My husband, my girls,
>   And my boy.

They are going to tear you down, old friend,
>   And I know now that I will
>   Never see you again.

It breaks my heart to know
>   That you are going to have to go.

Now this is "Goodbye", and I
>   Don't want to cry

Because when I lived in you
        I loved you so.

What have they done to you, Dear old friend?
        They've taken your porch off...Will it never end?

And they've torn out your insides
        Where I used to sing,

Where the children played happily
        When it snowed and rained.

But no child will play, no one
        Will sing in you again.

Next thing they'll do is tear
        You down to the ground,

And not a stick to remember you
        Will be there to be found.

I passed by you tonight
        On the way to what now is my home.

My heart gave a leap and I wanted to cry,
        My love for you will never end,

'Cause they broke my heart
        When they tore you down, old friend.

Teach Me To Do Thy Will

Teach me to do thy will, oh Lord,
    For this I earnestly plead.

Teach me to do Thy will, oh Lord,
    For this I truly need.

Teach me to be humble before thee,
    I need humility.

This is my earnest plea, then
    I will teach others to love

Thee, dear Lord
    As thou hast loved even me.

To live for thee down here
    Dear Lord

This is my earnest plea.
    Then go home with souls

I have won
    To live with Thee through Eternity,
    For you died both for them and me.

Room In Your Heart

Have you room in your heart for Jesus?
    Is it like the day He was born?

No room in the Inn for the Savior of men
    On the first Christmas morn.

If you let him come into your heart today
    He will come and dwell within.

He will love you and keep you
    Every day with an everlasting love.

And then he will take you with Him
    To dwell in bright mansions above.

Mom, 2005

My Precious Mother

As I knelt beside my mothers bed
        One night when she was sick,

I heard a voice say, "She is mine,
        And she's coming home real quick."

I loved my precious mother,
        But Jesus loved her best,

For out of this world of suffering
        He took her home to rest.

She said, "I see the angels coming down for me
        To take me home to Jesus,

Nevermore to sigh, nevermore to cry,
        To be happy every day.

To sing his praises in Heaven so bright
        Where it is always day, because
        Jesus is the light.

I'm going home to see him,
        The one who died for me.

Oh, won't you come to the Savior of men
      He will from sin set you free.

Then we will be happy together with Jesus,
      Our Lord and King

And live with Him through Eternity
      And forever to him praises sing."

(Quote by Eliza)
This poem was written on December 16, 1955, 19 years, 10 months, and 3 weeks after the home-going of my precious mother, for I know she is with Jesus.`

My Wonderful Shepherd

Forgot my Savior's love had I,
        And heard Him call in vain?

Gone astray on the mountainside
        I slipped and fell, and oh, the pain!

Then I called for my Shepherd,
        Oh, see Him quickly come

Over rugged mountain paths,
        Through vales with water deep.

He heard my call, my Shepherd
        And came after his wandering sheep.

He picked me up so gently,
        Held me close to His loving heart,

And whispered such words of comfort
        Then I knew we would never part.

Oh, how I love my Shepherd,
        Listen! Can't you hear Him call?

Oh, won't you come while He is calling
        Ere you should slip and fall?

I listen now to my Shepherd
　　And answer every call

As I should have done at the very start.
　　Then I wouldn't have broken my Shepherd's heart.

I am answering my blessed Shepherd
　　With "Lord Jesus, here am I.

Send me forth to the fields ripe
　　With harvest.

Let me bring lambs to the faith,
　　Dear Lord.

Let me bring sheep as well.
　　Let me tell of your desire
　　To save their souls from Hell."

Written 1969, inspired by the Holy Spirit

I Don't Deserve Such Love

When I sit down and think of what
  My Jesus did for me,

How he took all mine iniquities
  To the cross of Calvary,

I don't know why He should love me;
  I don't deserve such love,

That He, my loving Savior died
  That I, a poor, lost sinner

Should dwell with him forever
  In Heaven above.

Hot, scalding tears come to my eyes
  When I think of all the suffering
  My precious Savior went through.

But did you know, my precious friend
  He also suffered on Calvary's cross for you

So you, too, my friend, would Eternity
  Spend?

When I see Him in Heaven
    I will Him forever praise

For suffering on that cruel cross
    Throughout endless days.

When I see His pierced side
    And His nail-scarred feet and hands,

Why for me He died that day
    I will be like the angels,
    I still won't understand.

Written March 14, 1970

God's Child

I am God's child through Jesus's blood,
       Without Him I can do no good.

I love Him and I know I should,
       Because He first loved me.

Upon that cruel cross he died,
       It was for me and you He was crucified
       Your never-dying soul to save,

But he triumphantly rose up
       From the grave
       And went to God above.

We are to tell other people
       Of His most gracious love.

Yes, I've been bought with the
       Blood of Christ,
       No longer in sin I roam,

For Jesus paid my penalty
       And He made Heaven my home.

He will also wash your sins away
       If you will but come to Him

And ask Him to forgive you.
       He will make you pure and clean
       With His most precious blood.

Then you will sing and praise Him
       Just as all Creation should.

Jesus Loves Me

"Jesus loves me,"
  Oh, how I love that phrase,

Not that I first loved Him,
  But He loved me to endless days.

He gave Himself a ransom
  My soul He from sin set free,

Now I belong to Jesus
  Throughout Eternity!

On the cross at Calvary
  God gave His only Son for me;

A sinner lost, undone-
  He suffered untold agony.

My Lonely Heart

My heart was oh, so lonely
       Till Jesus took me in.

He told me how he loved me,
       Died to free me from all sin.

Now my heart is never lonely
       Since Christ came in that day,

Why isn't it ever lonely?
       Because Christ came in to stay!

Written October 31, 1985

The Separated Life

As I sat meditating upon a separated life, I heard Jesus say to our Heavenly Father, "I pray for you not to take them out of the world, but that you keep them from the world." (John 17:15) Then it seemed like someone spoke. (Maybe it was the Holy Spirit) "An egg is like unto man's will. You crack the shell, the shell's hard, then it breaks." Well, after that, I'm taking the egg for example.

All of us have separated eggs at one time or another and found that some shells are harder than others. We crack the egg open, then very carefully take the yolk from one shell to the other, being very careful not to let the yolk slip into the white as it's so easily done.

That brings me to God's separating us from the world. His process is about the same and we do not like it very much, so as quickly as the yolk slips into the white, our lives slip back into the world. And God cannot use us to the fullest of His will if we let the least of the world come into our lives. How can we be a separated people if we do as the world does?

When Jesus calls us, "Come ye out from among them and be ye separate, and touch not the unclean thing." (The worldly amusements) His word teaches you cannot serve two masters. How then can we as Christian followers, and true believers of Christ let the world see Christ in us if we are not in Christ? Here are some references. Duet 14:2, Ps. 135:4, 1Peter 2:9, John 17:15, Matt. 4:8, Luke 17:13, Titus 2:11-12, Eccle. 2:1, Tim. 5:22. (Noah and his family separately, Lot and his wife separately)

There's No Power in Demonstration

There's no power in demonstration,
    But there's power in the blood.

Come to Jesus for your healing,
    He's the one that makes it good.

There's no healing power in people,
    But they are used by Him today.

Come with faith that he will heal you,
    And you will be healed right away.

He is the healer of the body,
    He's the healer of the mind and soul,

He's the One who died on Calvary:
    Jesus Christ can make you whole.

Written March 12, 1970

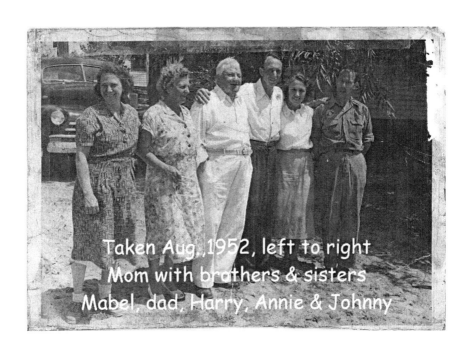

Taken Aug., 1952, left to right
Mom with brothers & sisters
Mabel, dad, Harry, Annie & Johnny

Obeying the Master's Call

We have all been happy together
    Here in this little place,

When Jesus Christ hears sinners pray
    And saves them by His grace.

But brother, sister, you are going
    Where we cannot see your face.

You are going to the regions beyond
    To obey the Master's call,

To tell them who are lost in sin
    Of the Christ who died for all.

Yea, He is not dead, but living,
    Living with God above

And you're going to tell them
    Of the Savior's wonderful love.

We are going to miss you
    But we know that it's God's will.

You are not leaving us forever,
    In spirit you'll be with us still.

And with our prayers to guide you
      There'll come to you no ill.

In just a little while
      We will meet you once again,

If it's down here or in Heaven,
      We'll praise the Savior of men.

Down in Peru where you will preach
      The living word of God

Which has proven so true,
      It's proven it's worth,

It's been Heaven on earth
      Since Jesus has given us second birth.

May the Lord, our God be with you,
      Give you many souls to inspire,

And we will see you in mansions above
      Where you will never tire.

Where we will see God and His wonderful Son
      And hear those blessed words, "Well done!"

On Calvary's Road

On Calvary's road I met a Man
    Carrying a heavy load.

I asked Him "What is that for?"
    And He said, "Just follow the crowd."

So I followed the crowd to Golgatha,
    I saw Him nailed to the cross

With an awful thud
    They placed the cross in the mud.

The very first words that he did say
    From the cross were,

"Father, forgive them, for they know not
    What they do."

He didn't mean only them, my friend,
    He also meant me and you.

For He was the precious Son Of God
    Who bore that awful load

And carried it to Golgatha,
       On that Calvary road.

It was for you, it was for me,
       That Jesus suffered and bled and died

And hung there on that cruel cross
       Till a Roman soldier pierced His side

And he pronounced that Jesus had died.
       My heart ached till it almost broke

When I saw Him hanging there.
       And now I want to let you know
       I have His love to share.

Telling the Wondrous Story

When I tell the wondrous story
  To the folks lost out in sin,

Tell them of the King of Glory
  Dying for lost souls to win.

I will praise His name forever
  In the sinful world below,

Telling folks to love my Jesus
  Who for our sins did to Calvary go.

When I tell the wondrous story
  Tears of joy do fall

'Cause my Jesus died to save me,
  Chiefest sinner of them all!

Christ, the Jew

To whom shall we preach the gospel?
  To the Jews first, the bible says.

Then Jesus says, "Go ye till all the world confess
  That Christ is everything we need.

Did He not the five thousand feed
  With five barely loaves and fishes two?

With spiritual food he will feed me and you.
  We must obey His wondrous word

And preach the gospel till it is heard
  By all the tribes and nations, too,

And they believe that Christ is Lord of all
  And believe His word is true.

And lean upon the bosom of this Christ
  Who was born a Jew.

Oh, come to me, the Savior of men,
  It was I who was born in Bethlehem's manger.

If you will come to the foot of the cross,
  Accept me by faith as your Savior

I will take you home forever,
  And you will never suffer loss.

Wasted Years

Oh, if I could only
      Bring back my wasted years,

The times I could have witnessed
      For my King
      Shall for aye I no trophy bring?

If God will only forgive me
      And fill my heart with His dear love,

I will to Him be faithful
      And win souls for mansions above.

United States of America

U-union
N-needs
I-instructors
T-to
E-educate
D-dropouts
　　To
S-study
T-to
A-advance
T-to
E-earn
S-salaries
　　Of
A-and
M-make
E-early
R-recognition
I-in
C-classes
　　In
A-America

America First

A-always
M-make
E-early
R-restitution
I-in
C-crisis
A-and

F-find
I-in
R-restitution
S-strong
T-ties

A Heart Like Jesus

Give me a heart like Jesus,
      A heart like His alone.

A heart where he alone shall reign,
      And He His royal throne.

A heart that loves where Jesus lives,
      A heart that in every way forgives,

A heart like thine, oh, blessed One,
      Then I will hear the words, "Well done!"

They led Him in to Pilot's Hall

They led Him in to Pilots hall,
　　　　With many stripes they beat Him
　　　　King and Savior of all.

And placed a crown of thorns,
　　　　Placed it on His head,

They pushed it on so far, until it bled
　　　　Then they made a cross
　　　　And placed it on His back

And each time He did stumble
　　　　The awful whip they'd crack.

Then they came to that place of the Skull
　　　　And nailed Him to that tree.

Thank God He died for sinners lost
　　　　For Christ has died for me.

But He arose one wonderful morn,
　　　　Oh, what a glorious day!

And He's coming back to take me
　　　　To live with Him for aye,

Oh, won't you let Him come into your heart,
　　　　Then He will take you home that day?

What I Think of Christ

What do you think of Jesus,
Who was born in Bethlehem's manger of hay?

Could you think enough of the Savior of men
To let Him come into your heart today?

I think He is wonderful,
And I know that He's divine,

But that is what I think of Him,
And I know that He is mine.

My Holy Bible

My Holy Bible is a book divine,
      It tells me of the great God's love

Who sent His Son, His only Son
      To be born to give us second birth.

He was born in Bethlehem so far away,
      In a cave on a hill

In a manger of hay for a bed
      The Christ child lay His head,

And when He walks in this sinful world
      He has nowhere to lay His head.

How can we get this "second birth"?
      By believing the reason He came

To die for us that we might live
      Throughout Eternity
      If we believe on His name.

And I know we should love Him,
      Who was born in Bethlehem's manger of hay

And tell others of His love for them,
        Tell them without delay.

I am telling you this day, my friend,
        Of this child who was born in a manger of hay.

One day they nailed Him to a tree
        To die on the old, rugged cross

To pay the price of salvation
        For you and for me

That we might not be lost,
        At what a terrible cost!

Rekindle My Desire

Lord Jesus, rekindle the fire of Thy love in my heart and grant me today that I may make it. Each day when I awaken, make it my choice to follow Thy footsteps wherever they lead, and obey thy sweet voice. For this end thy sweet grace each day will I plead.

He is Risen

He did it for me, He did it for you,
    He died for all to see

We were the sinners, He was the
    Only Son of God
    Hanging there on the tree.

Oh, how He suffered with nails
    Through His feet and hands,

And the thorny crown on His brow,
    He was laid in a borrowed tomb.

Three nights and days He laid there
    But something miraculous happened
    On the third day,

For Jesus was not there, for Jesus had risen,
    The stone rolled away.

My dad, mom (Eliza), sister Louise, brother Richard & me (Emily)

Serving Him

Greatness is found in serving,
      Serving is my delight.

When I'm not serving my Savior,
      I'm in darkness, and not in the light.

When I serve my Savior,
      I'm as happy as can be

Because I'm pleasing my Jesus,
      For I know He is always with me.

The Once "Crybaby Table" Turns Into the "Happy Little Table"

One day a friend and I were walking on a city street and it was near lunch time, and we were getting hungry. We saw a little restaurant. It looked very lovely as we stopped in, but all the tables were taken with the exception of one. It was in the back and in the corner. The waitress asked if she could help us. We said we would like a table for two. The waitress said, "There is only one table left, and that is the one in the corner where no one wants to sit." We said we would.

When we got there, we heard sobs coming from that area, and we saw water on the floor near that table. The poor little table was crying so bad, it was breaking in two. But when it saw me and my friend, it gave such a sigh of gladness it nearly broke all the way. It smiled as only a table can smile, if you know what I mean. It took the cloth and wiped it's eyes and said, "Thank you for sitting at me. The owners were going to throw me out, because nobody, but nobody want to sit in a corner."

Well, when people saw how happy Little Corner Table was, they said, "We want to sit up there." Why? Well, because it was the only happy table in the restaurant. So after that we could not sit at Crybaby table anymore because the owners had changed it's name to Happy Little Corner Table, and everybody wanted to sit there. It was once a darkened corner. Now it is so bright, people can see it as they enter the restaurant. People come from around the town to see Happy Little Table.

The Night I Met My Savior

I met my Savior Wednesday night
    So many years ago.

It was a wintery, stormy night,
    The streets were full of snow.

Inside the Gospel Lighthouse
    It was warm, and not so bright.

On that night, December 17th,
    Until Jesus turned on my light.

Then His brightness overwhelmed me
    When I found He loved me so

To buy my soul's salvation
    He did to Calvary go.

He Died For All

Christ died for us all,
      I believed it long ago.

I still believe He died for me
      And I want the world to know

That Jesus didn't die for me alone
      On that old rugged cross.

He died for all mankind
      So they wouldn't suffer loss.

Why Worry

Why worry about our earthly cares?
>Hasn't Jesus promised to provide

As long as we are faithfully trusting Him,
>And walking closely by His wounded side?

If we are trusting Him wholly
>What have we got to worry about?

His loving hand and His bountiful care
>Will cast away every worry and doubt.

Written 1953

Jesus Set Me Free

In sin I wandered far away,
      Until one night I realized
      That I had gone far enough.

That's when the Shepherd found His wandering sheep
      On a night that was so steep.

He picked me up and carried me
      In His great arms of love

And whispered such words of comfort,
      "Dear one, I died for you on Calvary's tree
      From this sin to set you free."

Come to My Jesus

Come to my Jesus, He's waiting for you,
      Come and no longer delay.

Bring all your troubles and heartaches to Him,
      Come bring them to Him today.

He will forgive and forget
      All the wrongs you have done

If you will come to Jesus,
      God's own dear Son.

He will love you
      And be your truest friend,

He will take you to Heaven
      For Eternity to spend.

Written December 28, 1985

Joy

J   Jesus loves

O   others
        And He loves
Y   you and me so

He, the Savior, born in Bethlehem
      Did to Calvary go,

He bore our sins upon that cruel cross
      That we sinners must not suffer loss

And that's the reason why my heart today
      Is filled with J.O.Y.

Telling others that joy
      Of Bethlehem's baby boy

Who was born in a lowly manger,
      To His own He was a stranger

Turned to see me standing there,
      Asked if I would share His cross,
      Then I would never suffer loss,

I whispered, "Yes" to Him that night,
    I believe in Jesus, the Way, the Truth, and the Light.

Oh, won't you accept that Savior of Men?
    Who was born in Bethlehem's manger?
    Oh, please, listen to the Holy Spirit's pleading?

For Jesus died that you might live,
    So please won't you, your life to Jesus give?

Put Jesus first
Then Others,
Then Yourself last,

Then you'll have a home in heaven
    When this life on Earth is past.

The Nazarine

As I walked along a country road
      One dark and dreary night,

I was alone on that country road
      When One appeared in the whitest white
      And walked closely by my side.

I saw the pierced hands and feet
      And knew it was my Lord, my Delight.

I fell in love with the Nazarine
      As my soul fell at His feet that night.

He picked me up with His nail-pierced hands,
      Held me close to His wounded side,

And whispered in my sinful ear,
      "'twas for you I was crucified."

As I began to tremble,
      And tears began to roll,

I felt the burden of my sin
      Begin to leave my soul.

And now I live for Jesus,
       The One who loves me so,

I'll walk with Him both day and night
       In the way I ought to go.

You, too can walk with the Savior of men
       If you let Him come into your heart.

He will brighten your way, turn your darkness to day
       If you let Him have full control.

The fullness of joy of His abiding within
       Will ever live in your soul.

Written 1938

Greatness is Found in Serving

Greatness is found in serving,
       Serving my Savior is my delight.

When I'm not serving my Savior
       I'm in darkness, not in the Light.

When I serve my Savior,
       I'm as happy as can be

Because I am pleasing my Savior,
       And I know He is always with me.

When Death Comes

When Death comes and takes a loved one
    And you feel so lonely and blue

Don't forget that Jesus is with you
    And will take your sorrow from you.

He will not only take your sorrows,
    But will give you peace in it's place,

And if you will truly love Him,
    One day you will see Him face to face.

A Man at My Door

A man came to my door today,
      His eyes were filled with tears.

He wasn't a man of forty-five,
      But a man well in his years.

He asked if I could help him,
      I said, "Just a minute."

I went upstairs where my purse was,
      There was only a nickel in it.

But I gave it to the dear old chap
      And thinking of my Dad

I could hardly hold my own tears back
      For his story was very sad.

Written 1934

To My Brother, Johnny

Thank God for a brother like you, dear,
  I mean it with all my heart,

We will always be together in spirit
  Although we are so far apart.

A Heart Like Thine

Lord, crucified, give me a heart like Thine,
    Help me to win the dying souls of men.

Lord, keep my heart
    In closer touch with Thine

And give me love's pure Calvary's fame
    To bring the lost to Thee.

K-Bib-a-Noak-Ka (or North Wind)

There was once an Indian family who lived in a village in western Canada. The father's name was White Cloud, the mother's name was Silvery Moon, and the little girl's name was Little Star.

One day Little Star got very sick with smallpox. Nothing could save her (No, not even the medicine man.) and she died. They loved her so much, even in death they could not let her out of their sight, so they buried her under the great oak beside the stream that she had played in. Every time they went out to get water they could imagine her talking. Of course it was just the water going over the rocks in the stream, and at nighttime they would in their imagination see Little Star playing with the other little boys and girls.

One winter night there was a knock at the door and White Cloud went to answer it. It was Ka-bib-a-noak-ka. He wanted to come in because he was so tired after working so hard all winter long. White Cloud at first refused. He told him that he was making the house cold. After a lot of persuasion, he was allowed to come in as long as he slept on the rug by the fireplace, to which he agreed.

It was coming Spring. With the Spring came flowers and the wind from the south. White Cloud and Silvery Moon had another child while Ka-bib-noak-ka was still with them, and guess who named the baby with what name? He did, and he named her Little Breeze because that's all he had left.

Written 1974

Mom and Louise
1941

Prayer for Children

Dear Savior, I've nurtured my children
    With all the love that I had,

And now there are grandchildren to nurture for thee,
    And that makes my heart glad.

Written 1974

Are You a Christian?

Are you a Christian?
> Do you love the Lord?

Do you take time out
> For God and His word?

Would you like to become
> His child?

Just come to Jesus and kneel at the cross
> Confess, repent, and be reconciled.

To as many as come to the foot of the cross,
> Repent and confess their sins

He is faithful and just to forgive,
> Oh, come to Jesus and live.

Are you a Christian?
> Are you telling the lost

Of the Savior of men who died on the cross
> Counting not the cost.

Are you doing all you can
> Leading souls to the Lord,

Praying every day
> And reading God's Holy Word?

Oh, What a Happy Night

Oh, what a happy night that was
    When I met my Jesus at the foot of His cross,

When he turned my darkness
    Into everlasting day.

He told me that He died for me,
    And if I would let Him, my Savior be,

I would live with Him in Heaven
    Eternally.

Since then it's been Heaven on earth,
    Won't you let My Savior give you a second birth?

Then you, too, will see Him
    Face to face,

Saved by his matchless,
    Wonderful grace.

Written March 16, 1970

Gifts Brought to Jesus

Bring your gifts to Jesus
　　No matter big or small.

Did He not bless the widow's mite
　　Above them all?

He doesn't want your money,
　　He just doesn't want your heart-

He wants your life to live for Him,
　　Then you will do your part.

Jesus, My Savior

I love thee, blessed Jesus,
  For dying on that cruel tree,

But not only dids't thou die,
  But again from the grave arose

To go again to our Father
  Beyond the starry skies.

Thou has't promised all who love Thee
  And obey the blessed command

To come again to take them
  To that Golden Strand.

Oh, why don't you come to Jesus
  And love Him as you should ?

Then you will tell others of Jesus
  Who for them shed His precious blood.

Won't you be a witness for Jesus
  Who died on Calvary's cross?

For all who come to Jesus
  Will never suffer loss.

He Saved My Soul

How dull the day, how dull the night
      Till Jesus came, came into my life that night,

Then Heaven's bells rang,
      And the angels sang

Of a soul that had come home,
      I no longer want to roam

For my Savior, Jesus Christ has made me whole
      Because He has saved my soul.

Written April 14, 1981 (a dull, rainy day)

Wise Men

From the eastern mountains
        Pressing as they come

Wise men in their wisdom
        To His humble home,

Stirred by deep devotion, hastening from afar,
        Guided by a star.

        Written by Richard E. Bath, Eliza's husband. (my father)

What If Jesus Came?

What if Jesus should come today?
>   Would you be lost in your sin,

Or caught away,
>   Lost forever in a Christ-less grave?

Oh, sinner, won't you come to Him
>   Who came the lost to seek and save?

Oh, come to Him while you are able,
>   Put your weary feet under the Savior's table.

By doing so, you will be worshipping the babe
>   Who was born in Bethlehem's stable.

The Family of God

I am the Lord's child,
       Jesus is my older brother,

God is my father,
       And we all love one another.

I have sisters and brothers,
       Black, yellow, red and white.

I love them and they love me
       Though we are not in each other's sight.

Some live in Africa, China, India, and Japan;
       Some live in America, the country where I am.

Some live in South America,
       The British Isles and Europe, too.

We love each other,
       And we all love you.

My Unworthiness

I am so unworthy,
      Why shoulds't thou remember me?

Why dids't Thou walk the Calvary road
      And die on that cruel tree?

Was it because of thy wondrous love
      To save lost sinners like me?

No Hope, No Hope

"No hope, no hope",
  My soul cried in despair.

Satan was laughing at my tears
  As I was sitting there.

And then I heard the sweetest voice
  That anyone ever spoke,

"You can take hope, oh sinner,
  If only you'll take my yoke."

And I saw Jesus standing there,
  So right away I stretched out my hand
  And He held me so close.

Now where there is no hope for me
  There is hope for my troubled soul,

For when I let Him take over
  All the doubts and despair left me
  For my Jesus has made me whole.

Thine Alone

Oh, Lord forgive me of my sin,
  Cast out any doubt my heart within

And let thy Spirit reign alone
  For truly, Lord, I want to be Thine own.

Thine alone, oh blessed Master
  To do with me what Thou woulds't do,

To work for Thee a little faster
  With the guidance of Thy Spirit

Help me love as Thou dos't love me
  And to give my all to you.

If You Want to Live With Me

If you want to live with Me
    In Heaven so bright and fair

You must deny yourself,
    Take up your cross and follow me,
    Then you will My glory share.

But if you deny Me instead of yourself,
    Then you I will deny

Before my Heavenly Father above
    The bright, blue sky.

Forgiven, Forgiven

Forgiven, forgiven,
     Oh, what a wonderful word!

My God has forgiven all my sins
     Through Jesus Christ, my Lord,

Who was born in a manger in Bethlehem
     And became the Living Word.

He went around healing
     And doing things that were good,

And teaching His disciples
     The works that they should do.

Now His disciples, Peter, James and John
     Are with Him in Heaven above.

We, too, like His disciples of old
     Should tell others of His forgiving love.

Written 1983 at Taylor-Wells Rd.

The Urgency of the Gospel

Does the urgency of the Gospel
      Mean anything to you?

After all, our loving Savior
      Jesus Christ went through?

What did He go through
      For you and for me?

He suffered, bled and died
      On Calvary's cruel cross

That they might be redeemed from sin
      And would not suffer loss.

They, too, could tell their friends
      Of the One who died for all
      Who gave life that never ends.

Written 1974

Dear Daddy

I wish you loved my Jesus,
     My Savior as I do,

Then we together with Him
     Will meet beyond the blue,

And friends so long, long ago
     We've known

Will be glad to welcome another
     Of His children home.

Won't that be wonderful to see,
     Our old friends to whom so long we said, "Goodbye,"

In our Heavenly home
     Just beyond the sky.

I think it will be glorious
     When Jesus calls me home,

And I'm gathered with my loved ones
     Singing praises to Him around the Heavenly throne!

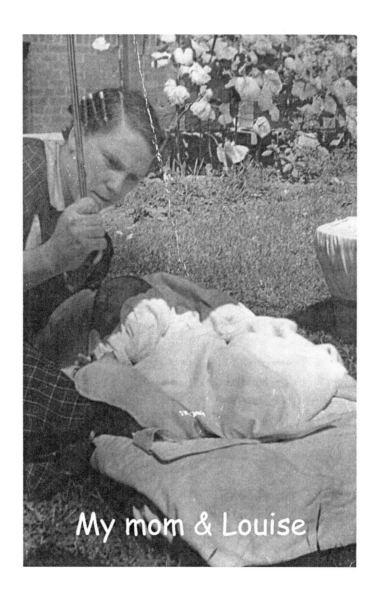

My mom & Louise

Eternal Separation

Eternal separation,
       Oh, what shall it be?

Death for all who reject the Lord
       Through all eternity.

The one who loves and calls you
       To His wounded side

And whispers in your sinful ear,
       "T'was for you I was crucified."

How can you reject His calling to thee,
       Listen! Can't you hear Him call?

And knocking on your heart's door,
       Why don't you let Him in,
       The One who died for all?

Then you will not be separated,
       But His forevermore.

For He will cleanse your heart
       From every sin

If you open your heart's door
       And let Him dwell within.

Written May 24, 1956

Town of Bethlehem

I love thee, town of Bethlehem
    Where Christ, my Lord was born

While shepherds watched their flocks by night
    On that first Christmas morn.

It must have been most wonderful
    To hear the angels sing,

To tell them of the little babe
    Who came His peace to bring.

And when they heard that wondrous news
    Coming from afar,

They wondered how the God of all
    Could have such wondrous love.

They saw a bright and shining star
    And followed it from afar,

They followed it to where
    The Christ-child lay

In a manger
    Made out of hay.

Telling Them of Jesus

Lord, if I loved Thee as I ought
      I would win souls for Thee,

I'd tell them of thy wondrous love
      That sent Thee to Calvary.

Upon that cruel Calvary's cross
      Thou suffered, bled, and died,

T'was for them and their transgressions
      That Thou was crucified.

Lord, fill me with Thy Holy Spirit
      That all the world may see

That I am not my own,
      But I am one with Thee,

Telling others of thy love
      And lead them to Thy home above.

The Stars Over Bethlehem

The stars that shone over Bethlehem
      Shine just as bright today,

Shining in the hearts of men
      Who see it's bright array.

Oh, why not let the Christ-child
      Who was born to us this day

Come into your hearts your souls to save
      This Holy, happy day?

He will pardon your transgressions,
      Christ will take all your sins away,

Then you will love Him as you ought,
      To Him you will give the praise

For saving your soul and making you whole
      For the rest of your days.

Let Go

Let go, and let God have your life, my friend,
      It's later than you think,

He will be with you to the very end of life,
      He will help you cross the brink.

You'll never be sorry for what you did,
      You will never suffer loss,

Because your life in Him is hid,
      Who died on that blood-stained cross.

Why I Love Christmas

Why do I love Christmas? Because my Savior,
      My King, was born that day,

In the little country, Judea,
      In a land so far away.

He wasn't born in a hospital,
      But on a bed of hay.

Praise God, He came to this sinful earth,
      Thank you, Jesus,

For coming and for giving me
      Second birth.

Why not come to the manger
      And kneel at the Christ-child's crib?

To you He'll be no longer a stranger
      Because for life what He did.

But He'll come some day as King,
      Will you stand before Him on that great day
      With your robes washed white,

Or will you be cast into darkness
      Where there never will be light?

Storms of Life

Ere the storms of life overtake you,
Come into the Haven of Rest,

And lean upon His bosom
Who has promised to give you rest.

He has promised never to forsake you,
Nor ere to let you fall,

For you see, my friend, He loves you.
He is Jesus, who died for all.

Written February 27, 1970, a stormy day

The Golden Strand

I shall not weep, nor shall I cry
      When my loved one says "Goodbye,"

He has not gone forever,
      For when I walk Death's shadowy vale
      I will meet him there.

Where we will walk hand in hand
      And meet Jesus, our Savior

And our loved ones
      On the Golden Strand.

He is Our Burden-bearer

Jesus alone knows our heartache,
      Sees our falling tears,

And whispers oh, such comfort
      Into the sinner's ears.

"Come to me, ye heavy-laden,
      I will your burden bear

If you will take it to My cross
      And leave it there."

He is my burden-bearer,
      He all my burdens have taken
      And cast into the deepest sea,

No more forever remembering
      The sins of my wicked heart.

Now I know that I am forgiven.
      I have taken Him as my Savior, and I will do my part,

Oh, won't you let Jesus bear your burdens,
      Come into your heart today?

And you will be happy in Jesus,
      And be with Him eternally.

Written March 24, 1970

My Heavenly Father

I have a Heavenly Father
    Who loves and cares for His own,
    I'm never, no never alone.

He wants me to take
    All my heartaches and care

To the foot of the cross,
    And leave them all there.

For He hears and answers
    My every prayer.

Oh, won't you leave your heartaches and care
    At the foot of the cross,
    Oh, come and leave them there.

There is no friend like Jesus,
    He loves you, and oh, how he cares,

If you will but come to my Jesus,
    He will answer all your prayers.

Then, in time of trouble
    You will never be alone,

Then you can take your heartaches and cares
        To Him who sits on His glorified throne,
        For then you will be one of His own.

And when He comes in the morning
        He will take you to that Golden Strand

Where it will always be morning,
        Yes, morning in that better land.

How do I know He cares foe me?
        He died on that old, rugged cross
        From sin to set me free.

He cares for you
        In the very same way,

Oh, won't you come to my Jesus,
        Take Him as your Savior today?

Oh, come to Him and be saved by His grace,
        Then you will see Him face to face.

Jesus Left His Heavenly Home

Jesus left His Heavenly home
        To make the old, rugged cross His throne,

For all who would claim Him
        For their own
        And love Him and obey His voice.

Remember, we didn't want anything
        To do with Him.

We, with the crowd cried "Crucify Him!"
        And that they did

And for your sins and mine
        He died.

Now, when you die, as we all must do,
        And judgment comes for you,
        Where will you run and hide?

If you come to this Man they named Jesus,
        And nailed Him to that tree,

Confess your sins to Him, my friend,
        He will from sin set you free.

Then you will not be afraid
        Of that dread day

Because Jesus has taken
        All your sins away.

Jesus, My Lord and My Savior

Jesus, my Lord and my Savior
    My Beloved, my Wonderful Friend,

I love Thee, my Blessed Redeemer,
    And will serve you till the end.

The King of My Life

I love the Babe of Bethlehem,
  The King of my life He'll be,

Why will He be the King of my life?
  Because of His love for me.

He came to Earth as a babe in a manger,
  To His own He was a total stranger.

Then he turned and saw me standing there,
  And knew that I would love Him
  And His cross I would share.

Alone With My Jesus

Alone with my Savior,
     What perfect rest!

Alone with Jesus
     I am blessed.

When trials and heartaches my pathway dim,
     I steal away to be alone with Him.

He takes my trials and heartaches
     He gives me peace within,

I then go singing victoriously
     Through the worldly noise and din.

Oh, how happy I am to know Him,
     He is my Savior and Friend.

So if you're sad and lonely
     Ask Jesus to come in and abide,

And He will come and stay with you
     And will ever be your guide.

Helper, Divine

Oh, Holy Spirit, Helper Divine,
>   Shine within this life of mine

That I might live for Jesus as I ought,
>   Telling of His wondrous love, as Thou hast taught.

Teach me to pray for the dying
>   And for those who are lost in sin.

Teach me to love the unlovely
>   For whom Jesus died to win.

Then I will be satisfied wholly;
>   Tell me, Divine Holy Spirit, just how do I begin?

I will deny myself, dear Lord,
>   Take up my cross and follow Thee,

And go where Thou doth lead me,
>   Through waters deep, and mountains high,

Through the daytime
>   And when the night is neigh.

Oh, the Joy When I See Jesus

Oh, the joy when I see Jesus,
    When I sit at His nail-scarred feet.

There's another joy awaiting,
    That's when my loved ones I shall meet.

We shall know our friends and loved ones
    When we gather around His throne,

When He calls me, I will answer,
    For He claims me as His own!

Written March 11, 1970

Bible School

Bible school is over,
       And we've had fun each day

Teaching all the children
       That came out every day.

We are glad to tell you
       Your children have learned real well

That Jesus came and suffered and died
       To save your soul from Hell.

Not only did He die,
       But rose again that day,

And some day that same blessed Jesus will come
       And take His beloved ones home for aye.

We want to thank you parents
       Who sent your children here

To learn of Jesus and His love
       Who is forever near.

And will stay near you every day
       If you will only trust and pray.

My Inseparable Friend

I have an inseparable Friend,
      He will be with me till the end.

I know He loves me,
      And when I stray

He finds me, picks me up,
      In His wonderful arms,

Where I know I am safe
      From all alarms.

Oh, separate yourselves to God,
      The One who loves you so,

And tread the paths that He once trod
      In this sinful world below.

If you love Him as He loves you,
      And do what He wants you to do,

When your earthly race is won,
      You'll hear those blessed words, "Well done!"

The Cross

Oh, if all would love my Christ,
        Not as I love Him, but more,

Then all would see my Savior's face
        There on that Golden shore.

His nail-scarred hands outstretched for you,
        He's telling you to come,

Come to Him who died for you,
        And He will take you home.

He is now with out Father in Heaven,
        Pleading for us our cause,

The reason why He had to die
        On Calvary's tree, the cross.

God Be With You

May the Lord, our God be with you,
      Give you many souls for your hire,

And we will see you in mansions above,
      Where you will never tire.

Where we will see God ,
      And His wonderful Son,

And hear those blessed words,
      "Well done!"

Serving My Lord

Fifty years serving my Jesus,
      Oh, how the years have flown,

They have been the most precious years
      That I have ever known,

Though sometimes I left Him alone,
      I have wept because He was gone.

But He was not the one who went away,
      It was me who had gone astray,

But when I heard His loving voice
      It made my aching heart rejoice

That He who died on Calvary
      Died on that cross for you and me,

And He's coming back some day
      To take me and you

To that heavenly place
      Where we will be with Him,
      Saved by His grace.

Written November 17, 1985

A Prayer

Lord Jesus, put a burden on me, only sustain me. Send me anywhere, only go with me.

Sever any tie but the tie which binds me to Thy service, and Thy heart.

Over Bethlehem

Hark, the herald angels sing over Bethlehem
    Of a newborn King,

"Glory to God in the highest," they sang
    While the hills of Judea with gladness rang

That Bethlehem night,
    Because Sin and Death had taken their flight.

"This is my body which was given to you. This is my blood which was shed for you." If Jesus loves us enough to give His life's blood for us, we ought also love Him in turn, to give ourselves over entirely to Him with no questions asked, to die for Him as He died for us.

Oh, For a Love Like the Savior's Love

Oh, for a love like the Savior's love
    Who walked on the shores of Galilee,

Oh, for a heart like the Savior's heart
    Which bled and was broken for me,

Oh, for compassion for souls that are dying
    Without the Savior's love

That I might have holy boldness
    To lead sinners to those mansions above,

For a great compassion for souls,
    And prayerfully watching for Thee,

I want to be more like the Savior,
    More love, more kindness to others I pray,

Till I love everybody and tell them of Jesus,
    The Truth, the Life and the Way.

Oh, Jesus, my Lord

Oh, Jesus, my Lord and my Master
  Fill me with humility,

Empty my heart from self and sin,
  That Thou alone may dwell within,

And I will win
  Souls, and Eternity.

The Friend Who Loves You So

I knew you'd come back to this little church
    Where I took you when just a child,

My Jesus told me you would, my son,
    For He is still meek and mild.

He still loves you, my son,
    Though you've wandered away,

Oh, won't you give your life
    To the One who loves you so?

He gave His life for you
    On that old rugged cross,

Now, please, my son, as I said before,
    Give your life to Him,
    So you never suffer loss.

Our New Undershepherd

We have an undershepherd
     Who takes care of his flock,

One who speaks of Jesus
     And has placed his feet upon the Rock.

One who leads us in the paths of light,
     Not through the vale of Sin's dark night,

But through the Holy Spirit
     Who'll guide your steps aright.

We are all God's children,
     And, oh, we love Him dear,

We have one who will tell us of Christ,
     That He is ever near,

And of that love He had for us that He did on Calvary die,
     And is now in Heaven above,

That you and I should love him who leads us with a loving hand
     To that better land of perfect love.

He Is Now My Lord

How can I doubt my Savior's love
     When He's done so much for me?

He came so long ago to earth
     To be born in Bethlehem's manger,

To die on that cruel cross for me,
     Who was a total stranger.

Oh, how could I have known
     For me He died upon that old rugged cross?

When I read in the Bible
     Of His love for me,

The story ever new,
     And yet so very old

That Jesus loves the sinner,
     And it was for me he died.

I saw Him hanging on the cross,
     And for forgiveness this sinner cried,

Then He answered, "Child of mine,
     It was for you I died."

I will not doubt Him anymore
     With His help and grace.

Then instead of doubting,
     I'll believe His every word,

And I am now His child,
     And He is my Lord.

Written 1981

My Wonderful Friend

Lord, I will be a witness
    In this sinful world below,

Telling others of Thy great love
    Wherever I might go,

Telling the sinner
    He is from sin set free,

When he takes the One who died in his place
    Upon that cross at Calvary.

Lord, I will be a witness
    To tell of Thy love for mankind,

That Thou dids't love them dearly,
    And left all Heaven behind

To come to this sinful world of shame
    The lost and undone of mankind to reclaim.

I love Thee, blessed Jesus
    For dying on the cruel tree,

But not only dids't Thou die,
	But again from the dead arise,

To go again to our Father
	Beyond the starry skies.

Thou has't promised all who love Thee,
	And obey Thy blessed command

To come again to take them
	To that blessed Golden Strand.

Oh, why don't you come to Jesus
	And love Him as you should,

Then you will tell others of Jesus
	Who for them shed His precious blood.

Won't you be a witness for Jesus
	Who died on Calvary's cross,

For all who come to Jesus
	Will never suffer loss.

Give Me a Praying Heart

To Thee, oh Lord, I bring my heart
      To cleanse and free from sin.

Come in and make Thine own abode,
      And dwell Thyself within.

Take out this stony heart so cold,
      Give me a praying heart,

If I may ask to be so bold,
      "Is this where I start?"

By asking for a heart like Thine,
      Then I'll be true to Thee,

Praying for others, my sisters and brothers,
      And Earth's whole family.

Written March 12, 1970

What I Think of Christ

What do you think of Jesus
  Who was born in Bethlehem's manger of hay?

Could you think enough of the Savior of men
  To let Him come into your heart today?

I think He is wonderful,
  And know He is divine,

But that is what I think of Him,
  And I know that He is mine.

Father's Love for the World

The world was in need of a Savior,
      Then God sent forth His Son,

Born of a virgin in Bethlehem,
      The mighty deed was done.

God's Son, Jesus Christ was His name,
      Had neither fortune nor fame.

He came to seek and to save the lost,
      Gave His life at an awful cost

When He died on a cruel cross
      To save us all from sin.

Oh, won't you open your heart's door
      And let the blessed Savior come in?

Then go rejoicing with gladness and joy
      Doing works the devil can never destroy.

Written 1958

Greetings In the Name of Christ

Greetings in the name of Christ
      Who was born on Christmas morn,

And is the Great Shepherd of the sheep,
      The keeper of the fold,

Oh, come let us go to the manger of hay
      Where Jesus, the Savior was born,

And kneel at the side of the Savior, so small
      Who will be Master and King over all.

Such Love

What have I done to merit such love
      That Christ should die for me?

What did He do that He shoulds't die
      On Calvary's cruel tree?

It was for the love he had for me,
      Not for the things He had done

That God sent down from Heaven
      His only Beloved Son.

Eternal Security

I have eternal security,
        You can have it, too.

Just bring your sins to Jesus
        Who died on Calvary for you.

You say you don't believe He died
        On Calvary's cruel cross?

In the Gospel of John, we read in verse twelve,
        Chapter one

That God so loved the world,
        He gave His Son to all who will believe.

Written March 10, 1970

The Sleeping Saints

They are not dead, but just asleep,
      Asleep in the precious Savior's keep,

They are sleeping 'neath a mound of soil
      Far from earthly suffering and care

Just waiting for Jesus to come in the air
      To take them to reign with Him for 'ere.

My Wasted Years

Here I sit in bitter tears
　　Repenting all my wasted years,

How Jesus Christ who loved me so
　　Could to Calvary go.

I took Him as my Savior
　　Many years ago,

But have I been faithful to Him?
　　Oh, no!

Oh, how I wish I could forget those wasted years,
　　I wouldn't be crying bitter tears,

For Him, me to forgive,
　　I would be out telling of Jesus
　　Who died that men could live.

Part of Jesus' Bride

Come take me home, dear Jesus
    Where I will ever be,

Close to the wounded side of Him
    Who died on Calvary.

He is not dead, He's alive today,
    Just as alive as when He walked in the Way.

I'm walking by that wounded side,
    He the storms of strife from me hide.

I love Him because one day
    I will be part of His bride.

When Jesus comes to take me home,
    And He's coming soon,

Oh, glorious day
    When He comes to take His bride away!

Written January 10, 1986

Judea's Hills

Far out on Judea's hills
       When all was calm, and all was still

Shepherds watched their flocks by night,
       They saw the sky light up so bright!

They were so afraid,
       Then and angel appeared to them

To tell them of the babe
       Who was born in Bethlehem.

Letter to Pastor

You are moving to Medina,
    May God bless you where you stay,

It is too far to come to worship here,
    But you will come back some day,

To see all your friends
    Who hold you so dear,

And when you leave
    We'll shed more than one tear,

Because we've grown to love you,
    But you will ever in spirit be here.

But if we meet no more,
    What a joyful reunion we'll have
    Upon that Golden Shore.

(Personal note)
I am sure this is the thought of everyone in church that knows you. May God bless you and be ever near you when you need Him. This is the sincere prayer of my heart. Your sister in Christ, (Mrs.) Eliza Louise Bath

Communion

As I sit around the Lord's table
      And partake of grape juice and bread

Representing body and blood
      Of my Savior

I think of the cross
      Where they nailed Him,

And the tomb He was buried
      When dead,

Then He to my awe-stricken mind appears
      As He did to many of old

In the garden,
      It's a story that will never grow old.

Then how my heart rejoices
      Hearing that blessed voice,

If you could and would open your heart's door to Him,
      Your heart would then rejoice.

You'd hear Him call your name,
      Then you would cry, "Rabboni," (master)
      He will set your heart aflame.

Dad and Mom
Richard and Eliza
1952

No Heartaches

We'll not have any heartaches
    If we are to the Savior true,

True to the Savior, first of all,
    Then, to our loved ones and friends.

Then He will save us from the fall,
    And we will with Him Eternity spend.

Jesus Took My Place

Jesus took my place
      That I might take His place.

He became the Son of Man
      That I might become the child of God.

He bore my sins that I might go to heaven,
      He became poor that I might become rich.

He was bound that I might go free,
      He went down that I might go up.

He tasted cruel death
      That I might have eternal life.

He went to Hell
      That I might go to Heaven. (Acts 2:27)
      He arose that I might have power,

Jesus took my filthy robe
      That I might wear His robe of righteousness.

He marked the books "paid"
      Because I could not pay it.

A Picture of God

A picture of God I have in my heart,
    A picture I never had from the very start.

But now that I'm in God's family,
    I have a picture of God and me.

He's holding me close to His loving heart,
    And telling me, "I will never depart."

And you see, that is the picture
    Of my Father and me.

You, too, a picture like that
    Can have

If you would walk with Jesus, my brother,
    God's Son, down that lonesome path.

Written January 8, 1986
The anniversary of my husband's going home
to be with our elder brother, Jesus, and our Father.

What Christmas Means to Me

What does Christmas mean to you?
>Trees, toys, gifts, and of course, old Santa Claus,

Well, you just turn those letters in that name,
>You will find that Santa and Satan and just the same.

If you teach your child of him, he will surely turn from God,
>He'll not trust the path where Jesus trod

Because when he gets a little older He will find out the lie,
>That you passed the Babe of Bethlehem by

To tell him of old Santa Claus
>Instead of Christ who laid in a bed made out of straw.

Christmas to me means Christ came to Earth
>To die to give us second birth.

That's what Christmas means to me,
>Not gifts, or Santa, or the Christmas tree!

When I Pray

Sometimes when I kneel down to pray
      I feel my Savior with me there,

And other times when I kneel and pray
      It seems that He's so far away,

But then I hear that loving voice
      That makes my wondering heart rejoice,

"Why hast thou wandered away from me,
      Thou knowest I'll always care for thee."
      Then I say, "Forgive me, Lord, when I stray."

Then in His arms He enfolds me,
      Holds me close to His heart of love,

And whispers such words of comfort,
      "Thou art Mine, for I have bought thee
      With My most precious blood.

And I will love thee forever
      If thou wilt be true and good.

True to me, to me forever,
      And good by keeping My word each day,

Telling others of my love for them,
      And I'll be with you all the way."

I'll be true to my blessed Savior
      Who died on Calvary's tree,

Then one day in Glory
      His blessed face I'll see.

Give Me a Testimony

Lord, make me willing
     To tell some soul that's lost in sin

Of how much you love them,
     You died their lost soul to win.

My friends don't seem to know Jesus
     Who died to save their souls,

To cleanse their hearts from every sin,
     And make them every whit whole.

Lord, give me a testimony
     For all who will listen to me,

Then I will be telling the story
     Of the Man who died on Calvary's tree
     To set sin's captive free.

Written January 29, 1986

The Cross I Wear

This cross I wear upon a chain to remind me of Jesus,
     My Savior, who died upon the cross for me,

And that His promise cannot fail,
     "I am coming back again," and when He comes

Oh, glorious hope to all who do believe
     On His blessed name,

He'll take them home to be with Him,
     Forever to reign.

A Life for Thee

Give me a life to live for Thee,
    A life that's from sin and self set free,

That I might tell thy wondrous story,
    And win souls for Thee, and a home in Glory.

Why I Believe

Why do I believe the Bible?
  Because it's God's Holy Word,

And it has the sweetest, most wondrous story
  That man has ever heard.

It tells of One who came from Heaven
  To die for sinners all,

Christ died for you and me, and ransomed us from sin's
  Dreadful fall.

I know my Savior's love is real
  Because He died for me,

You, too, can know the Savior's love,
  He also died for thee.

How do I know He died for me,
  My bible tells me so,

It tells me of His wondrous love
  And why He did to Calvary go.

The Friend We All Should Know

An old friend you knew well when you were just a boy
    Was at church today.

He questioned me as to your whereabouts,
    And why you strayed away.

I told Him I didn't know,
    But He knew the reason you didn't go.

But He wanted me to say,
    Because you are my son, you know.

He said, "Oh, the years I've waited to see Him here,
    The tears you've shed are not in vain,

Because one day he will come
    Back to this little church again.

Where you brought him when he was a child,
    For I am meek and mild."

Oh, how my heart would overflow with joy
    To see you talking to our Dear Friend
    You knew when you were just a boy,

It's Jesus, the Best Friend all should know,
    And our hearts with joy would overflow.

My Earnest Wish

My earnest wish is that I may
  Live for my Jesus every day

In such a way that He will be glorified,
  And others might see Christ in me
  For whom my Savior died.

He did not die for me alone,
  But died for sinners lost,

That means He died for you, my friend,
  Won't you take Him as your Savior
  Counting not the cost?

Written February 25, 1970

Help for a Friend

I was called to the home
        Of a friend so dear,

She called out, "Don't leave me!"
        When she knew I was near.

I rushed into the room
        Where she lay on the bed.

She threw her arms around me,
        And mine pillowed her head.

And she kept saying, "Don't leave me!"
        I said "Did you know there is one who never will?

You need Him, my friend, now that you are ill,
        The Christ who arose from the dead."

Oh, how I love my Savior,
        He hears me when I pray,

Oh, I would not be without Him
        Won't you come to Him today?

So I told her of Christ,
      The Savior of men,

The Lover of my soul
      Would make her whole again.

So I prayed for the Savior
      To save her soul,

Then an hour had past
      And she was made whole!

Live for God

Oh, separate yourselves to God,
      The one who loves you so,

And tread the paths that He once trod
      In this sinful world below.

If you love Him as He loves you
      And do what He wants you to do,

When your earthly race is over, you'll hear
      The blessed words, "Well done!'

I have an inseparable Friend,
      He will be till the end.

I know He loves me, and when I stray
      He finds me,

Picks me up in His wonderful arms
      Where I know I am safe from all worldly charms.

Written 1976

Lean on Jesus

Just lean upon Jesus, the Savior,
    For He knoweth what is best,

Lean hard on His bosom
    For comfort and sweet rest,

He will take away your heartache,
    Give rest to your weary soul,

Trust Him as your Savior
    And He will make you whole.

'Mom at her granddaughter Tammy's wedding'